Contents

Series Title 2
Discipline: Accounting 2
    Topic: Income Statement (and Trading Statement) 2
Author Background 3
Income Statement Explained 4
Capital and Revenue Expenditure 7
Identify the Item 8
Template for Income Statement 9
    Example 10
Worked Task #1 11
    Solution ~ Worked Task #1 13
Practise Task #1 14
    Solution ~ Practise Task #1 15
Practise Task #2 16
    Solution ~ Practise Task #2 17
Trading Statement 18
Introduction to Inventory 19
Template for Trading and Income Statement 20
Worked Task #2 ~ Perpetual Inventory 21
Worked Task #3 ~ Periodic Inventory 22
Practise Task #3 23
    Solution ~ Practise Task #3 24
Practise Task #4 25
    Solution ~ Practise Task #4 26
Practise Task #5 27
    Solution ~ Practise Task #5 28
Review Task 29
    Solution ~ Review Task 30
Income Statement Review 31
Teach a Topic Titles ~ Accounting 32
Further Teach a Topic Disciplines 33

Series Title

Discipline: Accounting

Topic: Income Statement (and Trading Statement)

- Want to get straight to the topic?
- Want material 'lesson ready' or 'student ready'?
- Teach a Topic does just that.
- This book covers the Income Statement and Trading Statement and follows this format:
    - Introductory theory
    - Explanation of terms:
        - Revenue
        - Cost of goods sold
        - Expenses
    - Difference between capital and revenue expenditure
    - Template for the Income Statement
    - Worked tasks and solutions
    - Practise tasks
    - Solutions to practise tasks
    - Introduction to inventory
    - Template for Trading and Income Statement
    - Worked tasks:
        - Perpetual inventory
        - Periodic inventory
    - Practise tasks
    - Solutions to practise tasks
    - Review task and solution

All you need for a two or three hour lesson on this topic.

Author Background

I am a trained teacher and have a Master's degree, diplomas in computing and belong to the Institute of Management. I have been a teacher/lecturer for the past 30 years: firstly nine years at secondary level then for the past 21 years at tertiary institutions teaching to graduate level. Over these many years I have purchased hundreds of technical texts. What I have found though is (apart from a couple of texts), I was probably only 'pulling out' one or two areas of information from each book and they have then just sat on my study shelves.

About five years ago, I finally decided there had to be a different way to approach each of my lessons. This is when I created topic booklets. Each booklet represents all that I need for a two hour teaching session: theory, worked tasks, practical tasks and solutions and a review of the lesson. Occasionally of course, dependent on the needs of the students, there might be a need to have another session on a topic – but again, I could use the same format but with additional practical tasks.

These topic booklets are my teaching plan/my guide – but of course it is equally important on how it is presented in front of the students. If the material is there and you are comfortable with it, then you are relaxed in front of the students. Dependent upon the discipline or topic, I still use PowerPoint and other interactive resources.

It is my intention to make life easier for teachers/tutors. If there is a topic that you would like covered; I would welcome suggestions and it would be my pleasure to create a topic book for you (so long as it was within my expertise of course).

Quite importantly, if you find errors in my work; or do not understand my rationale behind a concept – I would be most grateful if you drew that to my attention.

Note: For introductory concept teaching in this discipline, I have omitted sales tax (VAT or GST); as I feel there is sufficient learning with new concepts before introducing the 'applied' aspects.

I have taken great care not to infringe on other people's work; although it is hard not to pick up ideas and to develop from those ideas. Likewise, there is so much generic material that I have found repeated in a number of different publications. The amount of help that in recent years is made available on the Internet is a credit to the generosity of the people who provide it (both written ideas, tutorials, YouTube) and again, I have gained knowledge from these sources. However, if anyone feels that my theory or task storylines are too similar to their own – then please let me know and I will alter my material accordingly. I have purchased my own graphics software (IMSI) but occasionally also use free graphics from Google. Any drawings or cartoon strips are my own.

What I have found is that a self-contained lesson topic is what is needed – and that is why and how I have developed my 'lesson plans'.

I hope that you find these topic books helpful.

Contact Details:

Judith Pope
teachatopic@gmail.com

© J Pope 2017

Income Statement Explained

The income statement records all revenues for a business during this given period, as well as the operating expenses for the business. It is in the Income Statement where the Matching Concept is applied. This means that all the revenue earned in the accounting period is matched with all the expenses incurred to earn that revenue. It is only by doing this that the business can find a fair profit for the accounting period. The heading is 'for the year ended' because profit can only be calculated over a period of time.

I will approach the Income Statement in the following manner:
- Will deal firstly with the Income Statement for a **service business**.
- Will deal secondly with the Income Statement for a business that deals with **items for resale**.
- Will not include taxation, which means that Profit is before calculated tax to be paid is taken off. Therefore will use the term 'Profit' as opposed to 'Net Profit'.
- Will use the term 'Income Statement', but other terms such as Revenue Statement, Profit and Loss Statement, Profit Statement or a Statement of Performance can also be used.

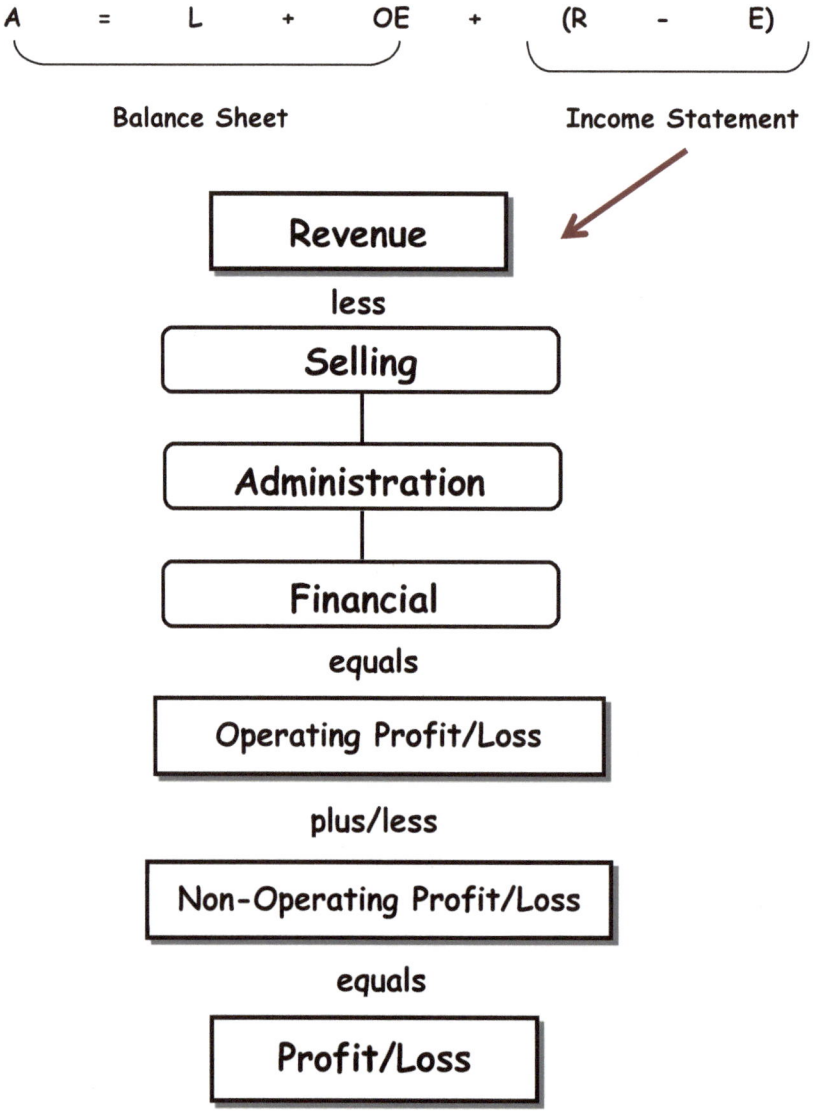

A simple definition of profit might be: revenues minus expenses where:
- revenue is the income earned from the day-to-day operations of the business – it may be earned from sales in the case of retailers, professional fees in the case of doctors, lawyers etc, commission in the case of salespeople or discount received from paying creditors within a given time limit
- expenses are incurred (or used up) in the day-to-day running of the business – and can include rent, interest on borrowed money, power, repairs, vehicle running costs, advertising, insurance, wages and salaries, cartage, postage, commissions paid to salespeople, cleaning, customs duty, office expenses etc

Cost of Goods Sold

Costs of acquiring goods and services with the intention of resale:
- cost price of goods, cartage inwards, duty, associated repackaging costs
- these costs are incurred directly in the acquisition of the goods and have a more direct influence on revenue than other categories of expenses

This expense is dealt with in the Trading Statement.

Expenses are classified. The classifications generally chosen but which can be adapted because of different types of businesses or by preference are:

Selling and Distribution Expenses

Costs of selling and distributing goods or services sold –
- incurred directly in selling goods or providing services
- are intended to assist in generating income for the entity

*Examples:
advertising/marketing
all expenses incurred with selling or delivery
freight (cartage) outwards
commissions given to salespersons
wages to salespersons/travellers*

Administration Expenses

Indirect costs incurred in the operation of the entity –
- are necessary for the entity to operate
- do not contribute directly to the generation of revenue
- sometimes regarded as overheads
- these costs are often the first to be reviewed in times of financial restraint

*Examples:
rent   insurance
rates   office expenses
wages/salaries telephone
electricity   accountant fees
repairs and maintenance
depreciation of assets
… and anything else that isn't obviously a selling or financial expense*

Financial Expenses

Financing costs:
The costs of financing the activities of an entity and may generally be classified as follows –
- interest – the cost of borrowing funds from external sources
- discount – the rebate on price of goods sold for prompt payment by the customer (designed to encourage prompt payment)
- bad and doubtful debts – consequence or possible consequence of customers not paying their accounts (regarded as a financial cost of making a credit sale)

*Examples:
interest paid
discounts allowed
bad debts
allowance for doubtful debts
loss on asset sales*

The more detailed analysis of the expenses that is provided, the easier it is to make performance comparisons with other entities.

While the Balance Sheet is a financial snapshot, giving you a picture of the business's assets and liabilities on a single day at the end of the accounting period; the Income statement is a record of its earnings or losses for a given period, usually the fiscal year. In other words, the Income Statement shows what happened during the period between balance sheets.

The Income Statement tells you or your investors:
- the income the business has earned in the accounting period
- the costs or expenses that were incurred by the business during the period
- your profit — the difference between the income and costs for the period

Revenue and expenses can be classified further to enable users to understand the relationships between revenue and expenses.

One example would be to distinguish between **Operating Income** and **Non-Operating Income**:
- Operating revenues and expenses are the day-to-day revenue and expenses directly related to the normal activity of the business.
- Non-operating revenues and expenses are revenues and expenses outside the normal day-to-day activity of the business.

For a cleaning business, for example, operating would be fees earned for cleaning services and expenses incurred in earning those fees. Revenue received for the rental or sub-letting of part of the business premises, however, would be a non-operating revenue. Donations made to a charity appeal would be a non-operating expense.

It is important to separate operating items from non-operating items in the profit statement so that an accurate view of the performance of the business can be obtained.

Capital and Revenue Expenditure

Before you can prepare an Income Statement or a Balance Sheet, you must make sure that you clearly understand the difference between capital and revenue expenditure.

Capital Expenditure

Capital expenditure is any expenditure incurred which creates an asset. Capital expenditure does not affect owner's equity. Any of the following expenditures can be classed as capital expenditure:
- purchase of assets
- improvements to assets which increase their usefulness or extend their useful life
- any expenditure incurred in getting an asset to the place and into the condition where it can be used in business operations.

Consider this example:

> A business in Chertsey bought a widget-making machine from a firm in Invercargill. The machine cost $12,000, freight charges to transport the machine from Invercargill to Chertsey was a further $500 and the cost of installing the machine in the Chertsey factory amounted to $400. There was also a $250 cost for the purchase of raw materials used in a trial run before saleable widgets could be produced. Six weeks later the machine developed major faults and the repairs cost $1,000.

	$
Cost of machine	12,000
Freight	500
Installation	400
Raw materials (trial runs)	250
Total Machine Cost	$13,150

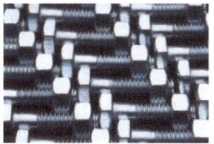

The amount of capital expenditure involved in the purchase of this machine is $13,150. Freight, installation and the trial run raw materials all form part of the cost and are added to the machine cost itself. The cost of the repairs six weeks after installation, are not included in the cost; because the machine was already producing widgets before the repairs were found to be necessary. Capital expenditures tend to be of a 'one-off' nature.

Revenue Expenditure

Expenditure, which is incurred in the normal day-to-day operations of a business. It involves any costs that are incurred so that the business can produce revenue from its operations. This type of expenditure does not create an asset. Since operating expenses are incurred in order to produce revenue, they decrease proprietorship. Each country's taxation ruling will set a limit below which an item is considered an expense. For example in New Zealand an item costing $500 or less is classed as an expense.

A business may buy many items that will benefit several accounting periods, but which have a relatively low cost eg builder's tools. Theoretically, these items are capital expenditures but if they are recorded as assets, they will need to be depreciated. Because of the small monetary amount concerned, the amount of work involved in this and the cost of keeping records far outweigh the benefits of having precise information available. This can be overcome by 'grouping' a number of items together – think builder's toolbox.

Identify the Item

Identify which of the following items/activities would be disclosed in the Income Statement and which would be disclosed in the Balance Sheet:

accounts payable

accounts receivable

advertising

capital

equipment

consultation fees received

machinery

inventory/stock

salaries

drawings

loan

depreciation

interest of $500 paid on loan

purchase of a vehicle

repairs to vehicle

stock purchases

installation of new equipment

customs duty

wages

insurance on vehicles

debenture bought

electricity

goodwill

bank overdraft

mortgage of $40,000 for building

fixtures and fittings

goods returned by customer

donations

cartage on new equipment

paid $1,500 to move old equipment to another part of the factory

sales

discount given to early paying debtors

interest received from a business investment

insurance payout to the business

cash

Template for Income Statement

Income Statement

for the year ended 31 March 2xxx

	$	$	$
Revenue			
Total Revenue			_____
Less Operating Expenses			
Selling/Servicing			
		_____	
Administration			
		_____	
Financial Expenses			
		_____	
			_____
Total Operating Expenses			_____
Net Operating Profit			
Plus Non-Operating/Sundry Income			
		_____	
Less Non-Operating Expenses			
		_____	_____
Profit			=======

Example

Here is an example of an Income Statement for Inky Inky Limited – a newspaper printing business.

Inky Inky Limited
Income Statement
for the year ended 31 March 2xxx

	$	$	$
Revenue			
Printing Charges			400,000
Less **Operating Expenses**			
Selling and Distribution			
Advertising	10,000		
Delivery vehicle expenses	3,000	13,000	
Administration Expenses			
Printers' Wages	120,000		
Office Wages	26,000		
Rent	12,000		
Telephone	200		
Postage and Stationery	1,000		
Electricity	3,000		
Printing Ink	1,500		
Cleaning Fluids	1,500	165,200	
Financial Expenses			
Discount Allowed	500		
Bad Debts	1,000		
Interest Paid	700	2,200	180,400
Profit			**$219,600**

Worked Task #1

Suburb-to-Suburb

Suburb-to-Suburb is a mobile electrical repair firm owned and operated by Jim Spark. Jim goes out to service items at customer's premises or homes.

Most of his customers are good in making payments but there have been a couple that he has decided just will not pay their bills and he will have to lose money on their accounts.

Jim has been in business for three months now and it is the end of the financial year. He has asked you – his accountant – to draw up an Income Statement to work out what profit he has made after all of his expenses have been taken off from the income he has received from his customers.

He provides you with the following list of account amounts:

	$
advertising	200
bad debts	400
van repairs	500
accountant's fee	600
consumables for repairs	450
repair fees	14,000
telephone	120
overalls drycleaning	300
van insurance	150
petrol and oil	600

What might be a more appropriate name to give to the selling expense category?

Complete the attached Income Statement template, thinking carefully as to which category of expenses each item belongs in.

Definitions for:

consumables ....

bad debts ....

Comment below on whether you think the expenses are realistic compared to the income Jim has generated from his repair service:

....

....

....

....

Income Statement for the year ended

	$	$	$
Revenue			_____
Less Operating Expenses			
Servicing	_____		
Administration	_____		
Financial Expenses	_____	_____	
Total Operating Expenses			_____
Operating Profit			_____

Solution ~ Worked Task #1

Suburb-to-Suburb
for the year ended 31 March 2xxx

	$	$	$
Revenue			
Repair Fees			14,000
Less Operating Expenses			
Servicing			
Advertising	200		
Petrol and Oil	600		
Van Insurance	150		
Consumables	450		
Van Repairs	500		
		1,900	
Administration			
Telephone	120		
Overalls Drycleaning	300		
Accountant's Fee	600		
		1,020	
Financial Expenses			
Bad Debts	400		
		400	
Total Operating Expenses			3,320
Operating Profit			**$10,680**

Income Statement

Practise Task #1

Sigmund Simpson runs a video repair business – Vogue Video Repairs.

He employs two people – one in the office and one in the repair workshop.

He sublets a small workspace to another business which provides him with additional income.

He provides you with last year's accounts to work out his profit for the financial year:

	$
interest paid	1,700
rent received	12,200
rates paid	6,000
insurance paid	3,500
wages – office	10,000
repairs	150,000
advertising	5,000
parts	20,000
wrapping materials	500
delivery van expenses	16,000
wages - workshop	40,000
donation (Braille Week)	250
interest received from an investment	1,000

Then he goes off on holidays!!

Required

Enter the above details into an acceptable layout for an Income Statement, which clearly shows the separation of income:

Operating
Non Operating

The separation of expenses:
Operating
Non Operating

A breakdown of Operating Expenses:
Selling
Administration
Financial

Notes:
- If there are no Non Operating revenue or expense items, then do not include those headings.
- Carry total figures across to next column.
- Never repeat totals.

Solution ~ Practise Task #1

Vogue Video Repairs

Income Statement
for the year ended 31 March 2xxx

	$	$	$
Operating Revenue			
Repairs			150,000
less Operating Expenses			
Selling			
advertising	5,000		
wrapping materials	500		
parts	20,000		
delivery van expenses	16,000		
wages - workshop	40,000	81,500	
Administration			
rates	6,000		
wages - office	10,000		
insurance	3,500	19,500	
Financial			
interest on loan		1,700	102,700
Operating Profit			**47,300**
plus Non-Operating Revenue			
rent received	12,200		
interest from investment	1,000	13,200	
less Non-Operating Expenses			
donation		250	12,950
Profit			**$60,250**

Practise Task #2

Amy's A-One Service

Amy is employed by local Albert Town households to carry out domestic duties. It is important for her to work out whether she is making a reasonable profit for the effort of getting out of bed each day!!!

The following Trial Balance was prepared on 31 March this year:

	$
Bad debts	350
Electricity	800
Insurance – public indemnity	1,900
Cellphone maintenance/fee	2,050
Petrol	1,700
Wages (for Liam to answer phone)	1,500
Donation to Plunket	100
Cleaning fees	14,380
Purchase of consumables	2,750
Advertising in The Courier	700
Depreciation on vehicle	200
Depreciation on cleaning equipment	180
Purchase of mechanical window cleaner	170
Discount (given for cash customers)	210

Note:

Prepare a fully classified Income Statement for Amy's business. Choose appropriate names for the categories – eg change Selling expenses to something that better reflects Amy's type of business.

Depreciation will be shown up in the appropriate category – for example which category will vehicle depreciation will be written up under – since the vehicle is used in accessing the customers.

Consider the total expenses for each area: is there an opportunity for reducing expenses in any way.

How does the net profit compare with the income received?

Solution ~ Practise Task #2

Amy's A-One Service
Income Statement
for the year ended 31 March 2xxx

	$	$	$
Revenue			
Cleaning Fees			14,380
Less Operating Expenses			
Servicing			
advertising in The Courier	700		
petrol	1,700		
depreciation - vehicle	200		
depreciation - cleaning equipment	180		
purchase of mechanical window cleaner	170		
consumables	2,750	5,700	
Administration			
electricity	800		
public indemnity insurance	1,900		
cell phone maintenance/fee	2,050		
wages - Liam	1,500	6,250	
Financial Expenses			
bad debts	350		
discount allowed	210	560	
Total Operating Expenses			12,510
Net Operating Profit			1,870
less Non-Operating Expenses			
donation to Plunket			100
Profit			**$1,770**

Trading Statement

If a business buys and sells goods it has to deal with the activity of this part of the trading before working out what their final profit is. There is an additional aspect/separate activity from the Income Statement for a service business. The calculation of the trader's profit is therefore done in two steps:

- gross profit is calculated (which is the Trading Statement) or the first part
- net profit is calculated (which is the Income Statement) or the second part

Note: 'stock', 'inventory' and 'merchandise' can all be used to mean 'goods'.

		$
	Stock at start of year	9,000
+	Purchases during year	18,000
=	Total goods for sale during year	27,000
−	Stock at end of year	7,000
=	Goods actually sold during year	20,000

Firm's Name
Trading Statement for the Year ended 31 March 2xxx

	$	$	$
Revenue			
Sales			67,000
Less Cost of Goods Sold			
Opening Inventory	9,000		
plus Purchases	18,000		
equals goods available for sale		27,000	
less Closing Inventory		7,000	
equals Cost of Goods Sold			20,000
Gross Profit			**$47,000**

Note:

The basic cost of goods bought for resale often includes two items which are part of the cost of purchases: Freight Inwards/Cartage In (cost of transporting in the goods which have been purchased); and Customs Duty (a charge levied by the government on goods brought in from overseas).

Introduction to Inventory

When a business sells goods to the public, it must do so at a profit if the owner is to receive a return on the investment in the business. This means that the selling price must be higher than the cost price.

As well as providing a return to the owner, the mark up must be sufficient to cover the other operating expenses of the business.

The gross profit is calculated from the following formula:

Gross Profit = Sales – Cost of Goods Sold

Cost of goods sold can be calculated if we have the following information:
- the value of stock on hand at the start of the accounting period
- the cost of stock purchased during the accounting period
- the value of the stock on hand at the end of the accounting period

Perpetual Inventory Method

Trading Statement
for the year ended …

	$	$
Sales		700
less Cost of Goods Sold		500
Gross Profit		200

Periodic Inventory Method

Trading Statement
for the year ended …

	$	$	$
Sales			700
less Cost of Goods Sold			
Opening stock	500		
plus purchases	750	1,250	
less closing stock		750	500
Gross Profit			200

In the periodic inventory method, the stock at the end of the accounting period is recorded as a current asset in the Balance Sheet.

Template for Trading and Income Statement

Business Name
Income Statement
for the year ended 31 March 2xxx

	$	$	$
Revenue			
Sales		_____	
less Sales Returns			
less Cost of Goods Sold			
Opening Inventory			
plus Purchases			
plus Customs			
plus Freight			
plus Adjustments	_____		
less Purchases Returns			
less Closing Inventory		_____	
Gross Profit			
less Operating Expenses			
Selling			
advertising			
freight outwards			
sales wages			
client refreshments	_____		
Administration			
electricity			
vehicle expenses			
depreciation			
telephone			
insurance			
admin wages			
postage and stationery			
rates			
accountant fee	_____		
Financial			
mortgage interest			
discount given			
doubtful debts			
bad debts			
overdraft interest	_____	_____	
Total Expenses			
Net Operating Profit/Loss			_____
plus Other Income			
discount received/rebates			
interest received			
rent (unassociated activity)			
interest charged	_____		
less Other Expenses			
donations		_____	
plus Extraordinary Income			
earthquake damages payout		_____	
less Extraordinary Expenses			
compensation paid out		_____	
Profit/Loss			$_____

Worked Task #2 ~ Perpetual Inventory

Cray Fish
Income Statement
for the year ended 31 March 2xxx

	$	$	$
Revenue			
Sales			413,000
less COGS			41,500
Gross Profit			**371,500**
less Operating Expenses			
Sales and Distribution			
packing expenses	3,796		
delivery expenses	5,487		
wages - staff	21,800		
electricity	12,400		
equipment repairs	968	44,451	
Administration			
insurance	5,250		
accountant fee	1,700		
general expenses	13,170		
rates	7,400	27,520	
Financial			
discount allowed	1,315		
interest on bank loan	2,250		
bad debts	350	3,915	75,886
Profit			**$295,614**

Worked Task #3 ~ Periodic Inventory

Decorative Floor Specialists
Income Statement
for the year ended 31 March 2xxx

	$	$	$
Revenue			
Carpet Sales	39,200		
Tile Sales	58,800	98,000	
less Sales Returns		500	
Total Revenue			97,500
Less Cost of Sales			
Opening Stock	1,900		
plus Purchases	65,000		
plus Cartage Inwards	1,170		
plus Customs Duty	1,050	69,120	
less Purchases Returns	4,200		
less Closing Stock	12,100	16,300	52,820
Gross Profit			**44,680**
Less Operating Expenses			
Selling			
Delivery van expenses	320		
Signage and advertising	1,425		
Wrapping materials	1,200		
Wages - salesperson	21,850	24,795	
Administration			
Rent	7,000		
Telephone	945		
Public Liability insurance	1,250		
Power and lighting	2,420		
Stationery	60	11,675	
Financial Expenses			
Discount Allowed		420	
Total Operating Expenses			36,890
Operating Profit			**$7,790**

Practise Task #3

The Green Stall

Mr Kabbs, fruiterer, is the proprietor of the Green Stall. He buys his fruit from local horticulturalists and sells it on to passing motorists from his front gate.

He provides you with the following information for the end of March this year and asks you to prepare an Income Statement.

Mr Kabbs uses the periodic inventory method.

	$
sales	4,576
sales returns	12
telephone	50
purchases	2,005
wages	180
interest on overdraft	55
advertising signs	42
purchases returns	70
delivery van expenses	82
electricity	100
wrapping paper	80
stationery	20
discount allowed	25
maintenance on stall	150
trading licence	217
consumables (buckets, trays etc)	168
food Safety inspection cost	170

Additional Information:
opening stock	90
closing stock	140

Solution ~ Practise Task #3

The Green Stall
Income Statement
for the year ended 31 March 2xxx

	$	$	$
Revenue			
Sales		4,576	
less Sales Returns		12	4,564
Total Revenue			
Less Cost of Sales			
Opening Stock		90	
plus Purchases	2,005		
less Purchases Returns	70	1,935	
		2,025	
less Closing Stock		140	1,885
Gross Profit			2,679
Less Operating Expenses			
Selling			
delivery van expenses	82		
advertising signs	42		
maintenance on stall	150		
wrapping paper	80		
consumables (buckets, trays etc)	168		
wages	180	702	
Administration			
trading licence	217		
stationery	20		
telephone	50		
Food Safety inspection cost	170		
electricity	100	557	
Financial Expenses			
discount allowed	25		
interest on overdraft	55	80	
Total Operating Expenses			1,339
Operating Profit			**$1,340**

Practise Task #4

Sail Way Boats

Dave Jennings set up a business in Lake Telopa two years ago, producing small sailing boats. Business has been steady in these establishment years with most of the boats for recreational use on the hydro lakes. He is hopeful that future predicted development will bring in further orders.

You have started your own accounting firm and as Dave is a mate, you offer to do his books for him (for a discounted charge!!).

Dave has decided to use the periodic inventory method since his business is small and the product is easily identified (for stock taking purposes).

	$
freight out	3,804
returns in	2,904
opening stock	92,705
salesman's travelling expenses	14,982
bad debts	1,962
rates	3,000
insurance	3,740
purchases	192,532
freight inwards	1,976
stationery	846
purchases returns	3,691
office expenses	7,844
electricity	1,185
office wages	8,000
general repairs	975
mortgage interest	3,271
discounts allowed	1,614
sales	352,187
advertising	431
wages – builders and salesperson	65,000

Notes:
- closing stock – $89,619
- Prepare a Trading Statement for Sail Way Boats.
- Prepare a fully classified Income Statement for Sail Way Boats.

Solution ~ Practise Task #4

Sail Way Boats
Income Statement
for the year ended 31 March 2xxx

	$	$	$
Revenue			
Sales		352,187	
less Sales Returns		2,904	349,283
Less Cost of Goods			
Opening Stock	92,705		
plus Purchases	192,532		
plus Freight In	1,976	287,213	
less Purchases Returns		3,691	
less Closing Stock		89,619	193,903
Gross Profit			**155,380**
less Operating Expenses			
Selling			
wages	65,000		
advertising	431		
freight out	3,804		
salesman's travelling expenses	14,982	84,217	
Administration			
office wages	8,000		
stationery	846		
rates	3,000		
office expenses	7,844		
electricity	1,185		
general repairs	975		
insurance	3,740	25,590	
Financial			
discounts allowed	1,614		
bad debts	1,962		
mortgage interest	3,271	6,847.00	116,654
Net Profit			**$38,726**

Practise Task #5

Betty's Bakery

Betty has a small bakery in Tollenton. She specialises in muffins which she supplies to the local schools.

She provides the following end of year information for you to write up a fully classified Income Statement.

Betty uses the perpetual inventory method.

Cost of goods sold	5,560
Commission received	200
Advertising	280
Insurance	1,400
Sales	71,420
Wage paid to herself	17,000
Discount allowed	200
Rent received on shed	4,000
Loss on disposal of dishwasher	500
Delivery expenses	1,700
Electricity	4,700
Utensil purchases	800
Vehicle expenses	975
General administration expenses	1,000
Interest expense	261

Additional Information:
- The commission was for a birthday cake she made in the normal course of her business.
- Cellphone costs are $110 a month (half is personal usage).
- Betty has a shed at the rear of her bakery that she has no use for – and it is rented out to a local pottery group.
- There has been one school that has been a poor paying debtor; and Betty has decided to enter them as a bad debt as it is too difficult to recover what they still owe her - $677.
- Betty pays $435 a half year in rates to the District Council.
- The accountant's fee for filing her previous year's return to Inland Revenue is $440.
- Betty was persuaded to lease out her kitchen to a local school for a fund raising effort – she received $2,800 for this but this year she also donated $700 to another school for their spelling bee competition.

Solution ~ Practise Task #5

Betty's Bakery
Income Statement
for year ended 31 March 2xxx

	$	$	$
Revenue			
Muffin sales		71,420	
Commission		200	71,620
less Cost of Goods Sold			5,560
Gross Profit			**66,060**
Operating Expenses			
Selling			
Advertising	280		
Electricity	4,700		
Delivery expenses	1,700		
Utensil purchases	800		
Wage - Betty	17,000		
Vehicle expenses	975	25,455	
Administration			
Insurance	1,400		
Cellphone - business	660		
Accountant fee	440		
Rates	870		
General expenses	1,000	4,370	
Financial			
Interest paid	261		
Bad Debt	677		
Discount Allowed	200		
Loss on disposal of dishwasher	500	1,638	31,463
Operating Profit			**34,597**
plus Non Operating Revenue			
rent of shed	4,000		
leased kitchen for charity event	2,800	6,800	
less Non Operating Expense			
donation		700	6,100
Profit			**$40,697**

Review Task

Wholesale Goods Ltd

Shown below is the Income Statement for Wholesale Goods Ltd. Unfortunately, it has several errors.

Find the errors – then rewrite the statement correctly.

Wholesale Goods Ltd

	$	$	$
Sales			129,450
less Purchases return			1,820
			127,630
less Cost of goods sold			
stock 31/3/2017		1,200	
add purchases		50,000	
		62,000	
less Stock 1/4/2016		7,000	55,000
Net Profit			72,630
Selling Expenses			
advertising	1,250		
interest paid	250		
commission paid	640		
computer repairs	420	2,560	
Administration Expenses			
wages - sales staff	19,500		
wages - office staff	18,200	37,700	
Financial Expenses			
insurance		3,400	43,660
Gross Profit			$28,970

Hints:
- Errors include layout requirements.
- You should be able to locate 8 mistakes (at least).

Solution ~ Review Task

Wholesale Goods Ltd
Income Statement
for the year ended 31 March 2017

	$	$	$
Revenue			
Sales			129,450
less Cost of goods sold			
stock 1/4/2016	7,000		
add purchases	50,000	57,000	
less Purchases return	1,820		
less Stock 31/3/2017	1,200	3,020	53,980
Gross Profit			75,470
less Expenses			
Selling Expenses			
advertising	1,250		
wages - sales staff	19,500		
commission paid	640	21,390	
Administration Expenses			
computer repairs	420		
insurance	3,400		
wages - office staff	18,200	22,020	
Financial Expenses			
interest paid		250	43,660
Net Profit			**$31,810**

Income Statement Review

As with the Balance Sheet, an in-depth knowledge of accounting is not necessary for you to make good use of the Income Statement data. The Income Statement provides the investor with much insight to the business' revenues and expenses. You can identify where the business spends much of its income and compare that to:

- similar businesses
- previous year's performance

Most importantly, the Statement tells an investor/owner if the business is profitable.

For example, you can use your income statement to determine sales trends. Are sales going up or down, or are they holding steady? If they're going up, are they going up at the rate you want or expect?

Also, if you sell goods, you can use the income statement to monitor quality control. Look at your sales returns and allowances. If that number is rising, it may indicate that you have a problem with product quality.

Gross profit on sales is important because it reveals the profitability of a company's core business. A company with a high gross profit has more money left over to pump into research and development of new products, marketing campaigns or pass onto investors etc.

Investors should also monitor changes in gross profit. For instance, a decrease in gross profit could be caused by an industry price war that has forced the company to sell its products at a lower price. Poor management of costs could also lead to a decreased gross profit.

Also, check out your selling expense. It should increase only in proportion to increases in sales. Disproportionate increases in selling expense should be followed up and corrected.

General and administrative expenses should also be closely watched. Increases in this area may mean that the company is getting too bureaucratic and is in line for some cost-cutting measures, or that equipment maintenance is too expensive and new equipment should be considered.

Interest expense is an important measure of how your company is doing. If your interest expense is increasing rapidly as a percentage of sales or net income, you may be in the process of becoming overburdened with debt.

Operating profit is particularly important because it is a measure of profitability based on a company's operations. In other words, it assesses whether or not the foundation of a company is profitable. It ignores income or losses outside of a company's normal operating activities ie non-operating income and expenses such as interest received, donations. It also excludes extraordinary events, such as lawsuits or natural disasters, which in a typical year would not affect the company's bottom line.

An easy way to calculate operating income is:

Operating Income = Gross Profit – General Operating Expenses – Depreciation Expense

Teach a Topic Titles ~ Accounting

- ≈ Accounting Equation

- ≈ Perpetual versus Periodic Inventory

- ≈ Income Statement (and Trading Statement)

- ≈ Balance Sheet

- ≈ Terminology and Concepts

- ≈ Depreciation

- ≈ Cash Flow Statements

- ≈ Partnerships

- ≈ Interpretation and Analysis

- ≈ Breakeven Analysis

- ≈ Budgeting

Further Teach a Topic Disciplines

- Accounting Practices

- Business Communication

- Business Computing – Intermediate

- Business Computing – Applied

- Financial Accounting

- Management

- Marketing